EASING THE GRAVITY FIELD

for Noreen

Christopher Stb,

Dec '06

EASING THE GRAVITY FIELD

poems of science and love

Christopher Southgate

Shoestring Press

Typeset and printed by Q3 Print Project Management Ltd, Loughborough, Leics
(01509) 213456

Published by Shoestring Press
19 Devonshire Avenue, Beeston, Nottingham, NG9 1BS
(0115) 925 1827
www.shoestringpress.co.uk

First published 2006
© Copyright: Christopher Southgate
The moral right of the author has been asserted.
ISBN: 1 904886 29 9

Shoestring Press gratefully acknowledges financial assistance from Arts Council England

ACKNOWLEDGMENTS

Thanks are due to the editors of the following books in which a number of these poems, or versions of these poems, first appeared: *The Methuen Book of Poems for Every Day of the Year* (Methuen, 2005), *Oxford Poets 2004*, ed. David Constantine and Bernard O'Donoghue (Carcanet Press, 2004), *Brave New World: Theology, Ethics and the Human Genome* ed. Celia Deane-Drummond (T&T Clark, 2003), and *Taboo* ed. Stephen Sims (Blue Button, 1993).

Also to the editors of the following magazines: *Acumen, Ars Interpres, Cider Press Review, The Crucible, Fire, The Flying Post, Otter, Paris Atlantic, The Reader, Third Way, Sepia, The West Branch, and Yellow Crane.*

The sequence 'A Suitcase of Letters' was first drafted on a Fellowship at Hawthornden Castle in April 2000, and I thank the Trustees warmly for their support. I also thank the centre 'Waves of Three Seas' on the island of Rhodes for their generous hospitality in September 2001.

'The Archive Room' was commended in the 2005 Poetry London Competition.

I am most grateful to the sculptor Peter Randall-Page for his co-operation both with the sequence 'The Stone and the Garden' and with the taking of the cover photograph. My editor John Lucas has been the consistently supportive, constructively critical voice that all poets need.

For the love – and friendship – of Sandy and Jac no words of thanks are enough.

Cover photograph by Frankie Fraser.

This collection is dedicated to the memory of my grandmother Lilian Depree of Parford, who is the main focus of the poems in the last sequence in the book.

Unto God we offer the work of our hands.

CONTENTS

I VARIATIONS ON A THEME

Falling Bodies 3
Woman in Blue Reading a Letter 4
Persistent Affection Disorder 6
David, Bathsheba and Jonathan 7
David and Abishag the Shunnamite 7
Scarlatti and the Lady Maria Barbara 8
Marilyn and Joe DiMaggio 9
Plath and Hughes 10
Ode to an Avocado 11
Love-letter to Helen Vendler 12
One Way to Leave Your Lover 13
I am always thinking of you 14
Meigle Museum 15
The Archive Room 17

II ARRIVING AT A PLACE CALLED POETRY

Arriving at a place called poetry 21
Fragments of an English September 22
Les petites entrées 23
A capsule falls from space 24
Christabel the Cat in springtime 25
A Note for Teachers 26
Jet-lag, driving, thinking 28
High Fidelity 29
Brendel playing Beethoven 30
Arvo Pärt's 'Psalom' by last firelight 31
Water-lily Triptych 32

III GIFTS

Madonna and Child 35
Gifts 36
The Upper Room 37
Foreign Mission 38
My soul like a weaned child 39
Carols at the Mental Hospital 40
Riddle 42
The Patient in the Corner 43
Funeral Wind 44
Mission Santa Clara 45
In Memoriam R.S.Thomas 46
Patmos 47
Iona 48
Lindisfarne 49

IV LOOKING EAST AT SUNSET

Crick, Watson and the Double Helix 53
Knowing 54
Sancte et Sapienter 56
Reweaving the Rainbow 58
Getting it right 59
Taboo 60
Memory 63
Wisdom gathered at Hawthornden Castle in Holy Week 65

V ANOTHER CITY

Amsterdam
    The Beguinehof 69

Boston
    The boy from Illinois 70

Chicago
    Last snow, Oak Park, April 2003   71
    In front of Chagall's 'Americas Window'   72

Granada
    Los Arrayanes, Palace of the Alhambra   73

Madrid
    Summer 2004   74

Mytilene
    On finding it easier to kiss Sappho than Helen of Troy   75

Paris
    Île Saint Louis   76

Rhodes
    Houses of bread   77
    The Artist of the Island Sun   78

Venice
    After Carnival   79
    Hicks's Story   80

VI THE STONE AND THE GARDEN

Poet in a sculptor's workshop   85
Two maquettes   86
Pulse   87

VII A SUITCASE OF LETTERS

A Suitcase of Letters   91
Love-letter from the Exeter Institution   93
The Letters   94
Insulin   95
Forms   97

The New Start   99
Fiammetta in her tower   100
Her Anniversary Book   101
Early journal and last letters   102
Coda   105
Flowers   106
My mother's Plato   107
A month after her death   108
Tulip tree at Glendurgan, autumn   109

I VARIATIONS ON A THEME

FALLING BODIES

After twenty years we stand on a beach
skimming stones. Your first, low, straight,
sets the pace. My last, as we turn to go
skips once, twice, tips on the breeze,
curves like a Beckham free-kick,
turns edge on edge through time-stopped air, walks
for a moment on water, sinks. A low sun
makes of the tidemark where we stand
a sheet of pale copper.
It is a moment I will want to remember
when I am dying.

We stand, Dartmoor wind in our faces,
looking along our own moonshadows
at a line of planets, longing to see Mercury.
But our eyes stop at Venus,
glowing, lovely as a throat-warmed pearl.
I know it is a sulphuric sauna
up there, a boiling ocean of corrosion.
I know the skip-stone obeyed Newton,
and Poincaré. I still add these moments,
reverently, to the worn and crazy calabash
we call our love.

WOMAN IN BLUE READING A LETTER

A young Dutchwoman, big with child.
We see her from the left, facing the light,
Clutching in her hands a single sheet of paper.

Vermeer has so arranged the space, the light,
The stillness, the shape of the face of the woman,
That our imagination streams to the paper;
We would like to snatch it from her hands,
To know what will become of her and the child –
Whether she has been blessed, or summoned, or left.

Good fiction would seem to demand she has been left,
That these fine chairs, this generous Delft light
Will not keep company with her and her child.
So we sigh, so we prepare to follow the woman
As she loses her looks, the smoothness of her hands,
Doomed to the poorhouse by the single sheet of paper.

Or we can choose what is on the pale cream paper.
We can summon the text from dozens of samples, left
Us by Mrs Woolf, Miss Austen, Henry James. It is in our hands.
We can suffuse the letter with the pure light
Of resurrected love. Or we can arrange that the woman
Is destroyed, by three short lines that speak of another child.

Such is our power, as imaginers. We give her one child,
Or two, or four. We send her the fine laid paper
From her lover in Amsterdam, or from the other woman,
Who also lives in Delft, third street on the left,
And hates her for the gentleness with which light
Falls on her young face, for the grace of those slim hands.

She is stillness itself. She keeps her hands
Close, almost resting on her blue jacket, her belly big with child.
Behind her is a map. Against its parchment a white diamond of light
Which is the folded head of the fateful piece of paper.
The map is of America. At its extreme left
Uncertain chartings of Baja California. Perhaps the woman

Is an explorer. So poised, studious, she is a woman
Ahead of her time. She holds possibilities in her hands,
Dreams of some Van Diemens Land. We are left
Any number of conjurings with letter, woman, child.
But she alone can be sure what is on the piece of paper,
For she has lain long with Vermeer, in that generous Delft light.

PERSISTENT AFFECTION DISORDER: A REPORT WITH RECOMMENDATIONS

Mid-February appears to be an especially
dangerous time. Quite elderly subjects,
some as old as fifty, jeopardise their health
on sexual activity, or fritter away
their resources on champagne and roses.

No regime of response is reliably effective,
though there are reports of success
using nubile decoys, stolen handkerchiefs,
or false reports of the colour of sails
seen in the far distance.

Sadly a proportion of sufferers
remain resistant to all treatment. They pose
a real challenge to our understanding. Studies
of the causes are inconclusive, though some
seem to blame Jesus, others a certain mythic boy.

The new statutory powers will allow incarceration
in case of a threat to society. Even this,
we believe, will not be enough.
We add the recommendation that all known poetry
be destroyed. Music, too, should be banned.

As a practical expression of our concern
a burning of the Song of Songs
has been arranged for today.
An oxy-gas furnace will be provided
for the melting-down of rings.

DAVID, BATHSHEBA AND JONATHAN

I had had various wives, by then,
aware only in myself of a proper kingly appetite,
and a huge yearning for the sound of his voice
that day he shot arrows, and I hid in the stone-heap.

Then I saw from the palace window someone content
in herself, in her own beauty, as he had been.
I saw it in the angle of her back
as she oiled herself on her rooftop, singing.

To get her I did evil, deserved and hated the prophet's
chill impeachment. I longed for straightness of love.

DAVID AND ABISHAG THE SHUNNAMITE

No, do not rise yet, dark one, last love.
Leave your brown limbs around me
a moment longer. A king's bones grow cold.
A king's sagged flesh, that once was taut as sling-cord,
grows sour and rots before your puzzled eyes.

Once, I would have wrapped you in vine-leaves,
and licked honey off each soft shoulder, olive breast.
But a king's bones... At night your hands frame my face
before your last kiss. Are you counting the days
of your safety? A king, still. Do not rise yet, Shunnamite.

SCARLATTI AND THE LADY MARIA BARBARA

Domenico Scarlatti composed over five hundred keyboard sonatas
for his pupil and patron, Maria Barbara, Princess of Portugal

Maestro, you are welcome. We were bored. What is it
You have brought us? *The light on the coins of gold*
In your necklace, and the argument of joy with fate.
But Maestro, your brilliant beads grow cold
From too much worrying, and still our death draws on.

I have brought Your Highness' horse, at a solemn trot
And shying at a bird in the hedgerow, and sun
Glimpsed through a waterfall. So play, Highness, not
Presto, ma cantabile. Intellect and caress. As though
To the love of your life. That will do, Domenico.
I will play. Listen.

MARILYN AND JOE DIMAGGIO

'Oh Joe, I sang to the boys in Korea'
How he loved that breathlessness in her voice
and how she'd come to bed
wearing nothing but the Yankees hat
in which he'd hit fifty-six games straight
and won nine World Series.

'When I sang in Korea
you just can't believe
how people cheered.
Joe, you can't imagine.'

Arms flung in the air
then sending the hat skimming
into the closet.

How he wished she'd stretch her agile mind
past cult figures
and her own applause.
He'd known applause.
He only wanted love
and clear signals.

And he said,
'honey' –
the moment of making
the straightforward play,
the moment of the final out -
'honey, I think I can.'

PLATH AND HUGHES

It was an astrological power, a ghost out of a well
or a bullet out of nowhere, or a prefigured
fate. Hers was an easeful sleep
in Heptonstall, his a hooded stare
into decades of wondering. It was Nemesis.

Or it was a dull case of sex-drives, and power-
struggles, and at the wrong moment an exotic dreamer
blowing through a ménage of poets,
young children, hard-made work,
and self-hate. It was betrayal, and household gas.

ODE TO AN AVOCADO

Your outside is an old wine-cask
bulging with the ferment of its cargo.
Nothing prepares us
for the sweet green sleaze of you
for your liquidness on the tongue
or how your ogive stone glistens
like new-stripped silk.

Forget bathing in milk, or champagne,
it's your sleekness in which
I want to soak my beloved
then lick her skin slowly
savouring you
with just a tincture
of balsamic.

LOVE-LETTER TO HELEN VENDLER

After hearing a CD of her reading some of the sonnets of Shakespeare

You ride with me in my car, enunciating
sonnets by number. At the lights
if the computer is against me
I can listen to you compare me to a summer's day
and still have space to savour the sestet.
In traffic it is the couplet's twist that satisfies;
on a high-speed bend a single phrase
gives life to time
                              as these lines
give my love to you, Professor Vendler, for the way
you have me stopping nowhere in particular,
frittering away quality time
on your fourteen-line incantations
to other lovers you never knew.

You are copyright the President and Fellows of Harvard College,
but in the car, on the slip-road, in the lay-by,
you are my clear-cadenced companion,
my co-conspirator in giving iambic shape
to unappointed moments.
                              In my mind
we talk on, of the need for form,
of Shakespeare's liberties with stress.
I tell you shyly
how my diesel-commuting life is lightened
by your grace of tone, and that I hear
your longing to answer Shakespeare back,
to take him to task over dinner,
to stop his mouth with kisses.

I hear it, Helen Vendler; I know
the form of that longing,
and share it gladly.

ONE WAY TO LEAVE YOUR LOVER

(with thanks to Paul Simon)

A National Park bear
treed by tourists.
Its warden
matter-of-fact as a noticeboard
orders us to remain quiet
and allow the bear to leave.

There must be fifty ways to leave your lover.

But here's one:
sliding, claws extended, ripping bark,
backwards down the tree of her trust.
Then sloping off
with the odd disgusted over-the-shoulder glance
treading heavily on meadow orchids.

I AM ALWAYS THINKING OF YOU

though blindness has made life
so difficult. I go through the motions
the Meals on Wheels. Thank you for the cushion
with my initials picked out
in heavy thread. In my dreams
we go hunting with the Prince
and ride together till evening.

We docked at Rhodes, in the era of Mussolini.
It seems like yesterday – no, closer,
the jack-booted carabinieri,
that Turkish garden
where we sat by the fountain.
The chiropodist today, fussy woman.
You always had such beautiful feet.

The house is in good heart.
If you were here
you would fill it with flowers.

Church tomorrow. In Malta
the Christian people prayed to Allah.
Here the Rector prays for us, to the God
whose indifferent property we are.
I hope you say your prayers
as I taught you
when you were three.

I am always thinking of you.
I know it is hard for you to visit
now the doctors won't let you drive
but somehow hope
you could be here for my birthday
and read me the thing
from the Queen.

MEIGLE MUSEUM

Only there, in the gateway,
did we touch. My arm, hesitant,
lifted to her shoulder.
Hers to my waist.
So, simply, things altered.
We paid and went in, to see the Pictish stones.

Twenty years later I was there again,
allegedly to look at Pictish stones.

I hardly saw them that first time,
watching her sketch the carving,
listening to her gladness
at finding them. My eye moved
between stone and drawing, memorised the line of her wrist.
She drew a camel and a seahorse.

I expected little, going back there,
except some odd-shaped Celtic curiosities.

In a village shop we were taken
for honeymooners. To her huge amusement.
The taste of her mouth, laughing, was
honey and cigarettes.
Her sudden tears were brushed away
with something I didn't catch, about transience.

The carvings are eighth century, at latest,
Celtic crosses bolted to the heart of the stone.

Those weeks were woman-scent and man-scent,
incense, and wine tasting of quinces,
and having to know about John Donne
as well as differentials,
a woman's moods
as well as molecular orbitals.

The wind at the gateway was as chill
as I remembered. Smelling of rain on the hills.

On the reverse of the main cross
were camel and seahorse,
salmon and bull,
and many forms that never grew and flourished
except in yearning – part-horse, part-fish,
part-otter, part-cat with long abrasive claws.

I expected to lose her, and did,
to someone older, and less anxious.

What I never expected was to be so moved
after so long, by the shapes that had moved her,
by fantasy side by side with authenticity.
Or to be so grateful for John Donne,
and the seahorse,
and the wind off the hills.

THE ARCHIVE ROOM

I move the acid-free bookmark to a later place.
I note, with the sharpened pencil provided,
the date of edition, printer's font,
dedication to His Grace.
                          But who laid the feather,
white, fine-filamented gift
on the title page? In what garden
did he give it her?
                    What stemmed in secret
from the gift given and received?
Why did she leave, on that other page, a hundred pages in,
at the description of the calling of a saint
a sprig of dried lilac?

She had to hide the love
            that trembled to touch
                        could not help but touch
the beloved, the love that ran its fingers
            through his fine hair
                        phoned at the wrong time, wrote poems
                                    to his shoulders, his wrists,
                                                his soul, was soon over,
was remembered always.

He was at a creative writing class
            where significant objects
                        were circulated as writing starters
and stole two
            tucking them between different leaves
                        of a book also stolen
later returned to the archive
            after the medication stabilised.

They were spies
        and used the words
                he after the feather
                        she after the lilac
                                to encipher
                                        national betrayals.
It was simply, between saints,
        that she placed the feather
                to recall him to the vision of Hildegard
and he the lilac
        to quote to her the heart stiffening
                for Ash Wednesday.

From the acid-free air
of the Archive Room
I inhale the answers
and write them gratefully
in that sharpened air
with the pencil provided.

II ARRIVING AT A PLACE CALLED POETRY

ARRIVING AT A PLACE CALLED POETRY

for Jackie Kay

Begin at Olympus,
or the Finland Station.
The ticket will cost you everything.

Notice whatever crosses your path –
how the haze hangs
over dreamed-of hills

how the platform crow
tearing at the cast-off bag from Burger King
rips the flesh of martyrs.

Endure false destinations –
dragons of the derivative,
tyrannies of prose.

Sing – as though long
smouldering anger
had never been sung before.

Love – as though the world's face
was a wee cheeky child's
upturned for your kiss.

Expect no banners of welcome.
Alight promptly.
Tell Calliope the drinks are on her.

FRAGMENTS OF AN ENGLISH SEPTEMBER

for Paul and Helen

Sleek light on the meadows
after heavy dew, the last mist
dispelled by glow of morning.

Mattins taken by a priest in his eighties,
shuffling stubbornly through pain
to declaim the liturgy
as though it were life itself.

Our walk up into the wind
at Cadbury, taking in the grain
of everything.

A small boy's question
about an acorn,
a frost-felled beech
aimed at Dartmoor.

This Michaelmas clarity
which puts doubt's angels briefly to flight.
A high gilt weather-vane, pointing west.

LES PETITES ENTRÉES

Memory halts the spiral stair
milkily picks out a butterfly,
deals, as every day, its cards, its jewels,
adjusts, as every day, outworn glories
on the hall table –
astrakhan, malacca, chamois.

As a small child he had a door
held open for him by Swinburne.
As a young man, darkly handsome,
he played a doubles with Lenglen –
let her down badly in the third.
Later he talked with the Prince
and the Archbishop of York –
just for two minutes, and
ran out of things to say.

But he rehearses still, the bowl
of his life lifted
to inspect its milky pearls,
the thin paste with faded lettering
from the Austro-Hungarian Legation,
the brief handshake
of the young Richard Nixon.

He is not wanted now to open fetes
or read the Christmas lesson.
Each day he takes out his will,
and has it read to him,
and drinks a pint of Dom Pérignon.
It is the one true satisfaction of his life.

A CAPSULE FALLS FROM SPACE

A dream

A capsule falls from space.
In liquid-crystal characters it traces out
'BEWARE THE MAGGON, SPURN THE GRANTHAM GROCER'S
DAUGHTER.'
And then
'SPACETRAK APOLOGISE FOR THE DELAY IN THE ARRIVAL OF
THIS CAPSULE
AND REGRET ANY INCONVENIENCE CAUSED.'

Another,
Hard on the heels of the first.
'ALL CAPSULES ARE LIARS.'
Ah, so chic, so deconstructed,
The extraterrestrials of today
Or whenever it was.

A third.
'QUALITY ASSURANCE PROCEDURES
RELATING TO THE RECEIPT OF CAPSULES
APPLY IN YOUR CASE. THE ASSESSORS
WILL VISIT YOUR PLANET
NOT LATER THAN 3005.'

'IN THE MEANTIME
A CONTINENT-LOAD OF DOCUMENTATION
MUST BE PREPARED.'
I go back to sleep, reassured.
3004 will be time enough to tackle
That particular planetary crisis.

CHRISTABEL THE CAT IN SPRINGTIME

On the window-sill,
commentating on birds,
our cat.
She has made of them
a lifelong study.
She beats time
to their sweet spring hoppings
with heavy bunts of her tail.
Cat-teeth chatter gently,
miming the grinding of bones.

When the impudentest
great tit has gone
she stretches,
considering some new
amusement. Then draws back –
reticulating her limbs
as smoothly as a lover
withdrawing a silk favour
from a balcony –
nods wisely, sleeps.

A NOTE FOR TEACHERS

Bluebirds drift off branches,
imitating leaves,
then flare upwards
glowing with light.

Later, in the Hard Back Café,
two women,
professor and student,
talking past matching laptops.

The teacher is expansive,
maps out plans,
graduate school,
what they might *do* together.

I cannot decide if it is
that she is in love with the rimless glasses
so coolly poised there,
taking her in,

or just that she
has a vast need
to see her own story
replayed in another.

The student's gaze
flicks to her screen-saver, flicks away;
her flawless hands start to attend
to her split ends.

I catch the teacher's eye, beam a message
(telepathy rusty)
into the hypercaffeinated ether
of the Hard Back Café.

You are the force of gravity
and air resistance
playing on the surface of the leaf.
She is the bluebird.
Savour the brief moment
of mimetic flight.

Do not seek to hold her,
or to rise
in her flare of colour.
Do not seek to save her to disk.

JET-LAG, DRIVING, THINKING

Heading east out of San Francisco
up into the Central Valley – hours of it,
though it looked like nothing on the airline map –
things come to me.

One – you've got to have noise
on the long stretches of highway
as you weave through the trucks for hour after hour
of fruit groves, brown hills, one-street towns.

Two – Mexican music, or bible-stations, are best.
The symphonies of Schubert
brought to you on NPR by Budweiser,
need the chic city to make themselves heard.

Three – wind generators can be parables –
can break through the surfed sermons
and the carboned fandangos:

driving up out of a canyon
into a suddenly singing sky
and a new expanse of valley

I see the great bird-blades stud the slope,
spin and slow, spin on another breeze,
lose heart as others outspin them.

Trucks and timezones pass away as I watch the blades,
watch my life,
out on the hill, listening..

HIGH FIDELITY

The man sits above the tracks
at Bristol Parkway. He drinks tea,
studies the distance.
He notes the numbers of trains.

With the binocs he picks them out
on the long curve from Scotland,
the hard-driving run from Swindon.
He watches till the grey light fades.

He drinks tea and talks to himself
about the rude girls who serve him.
He takes some pills – perhaps the ones
the doctors make him take.

I note him down,
after my airport poems,
my studies of Sappho, Bathsheba,
and Sylvia Plath.

I ride one of his numbers home
impatient to be undisturbed with a malt
and my rank-ordering of all available versions
of the Goldberg Variations,

BWV988.

BRENDEL PLAYING BEETHOVEN

written in honour of the pianist's seventieth birthday, 2001

At first each impact seems placed slowly, precisely,
like dictation from God. All is calm,
though the fireflies take shelter.

Each raindrop is itself, is swept away by itself
by a reprise of itself until the reprise of that
begins to batter at the lily-pads

They are battered by a pattern dissolved in a pattern
until the surface fumes, seethes, suffused by wounds,
settles suddenly to a dark glass.

Too soon an empty sunlight.
We whip up a commotion in our branches
Encore! Encore! The whole garden has need of this.

ARVO PÄRT'S 'PSALOM' BY LAST FIRELIGHT

Notes trying for phrases, trying for purpose
on a river of silence.
The cats' ears pricked, shifting
at tonalities. My eyes fixed
on embers. A high violin
stretches out notes,
questioning, praying.

The last coals are distinct now,
each glow surging from end to end
as if searching for a way
to perpetuate itself, then
subsiding into greyness.
The cats like statues of themselves
watch for the moment
when they'll become invisible.
Notes strain for silence.

31

WATER-LILY TRIPTYCH

Sitting quiet for a long time with the water-lilies
I begin to notice what must be the shadow of a tree.
Then the young Japanese girl along the bench
asks me if those puffy shapes
are meant to be clouds.
      I concede cautiously
that they might be clouds
reflected in the pond at Giverny
towards evening, at a certain time of year.

All I can see is joy
and after that paint –
paint swirling in cream-coloured crescents
to drift away like woodsmoke,
paint in bursts like a firework flash,
in liquid loops, sea-coloured,
drawing light down canvas.
Paint in rust-brown versions
of pipe-dreams.

They say that Monet, by the end,
was a broken man with degenerative double cataract;
that he could hardly see
his lily-pond.
     I say that when they propped him
into a painting-chair,
the chair his strength, limbs his penance,
all he could do was see.
And what he saw

was woodsmoke, thought, and memory,
joy
in all its abundance.

III GIFTS

.

MADONNA AND CHILD

from 'Transcriptions' – a series of drawings by Dennis Creffield

Madonna, and the swaddled child on the angle
of her arm, are one shape, an icon
of wholeness. The mother, a young Semitic
girl, wears black, her tenderness already
includes mourning. The child stirs.

                                      The angles
                      of the icon
            of the mother
               in black
are those of Pietà.

                    The child
on her arm
is wholeness.
        He receives our tenderness
                        impatiently.

Madonna
       arms clasping.
                   A young Semitic
girl, shy, frightened.
           The child comforting her.

          Swaddled
    we can talk of unions –
the Earth as great Mother.
          May the darkness of God
            make us stir,

proclaim the love the child has been to us.

GIFTS

First let it be clear – no gift is simple. For our part
We offered a nuanced disaffection
Well-versed in the French theorists.

In a ludic nod at tradition
We brought gold, in an ebony casket,
Little gilt line-cutters, and a useful box.

We brought incense in silver-studded teak
For the long swing of thurible,
The rise of ritual towards unknowing.

We brought myrrh in alabaster.
We made a significant investment
In the equipment of lamentation.

And we were there
So others said
When it counted.

We had brought texts, and a fine air-nozzle
Wonderful for cleaning celluloid
And dusting the pollen from lilies.

We waited thirty years.

And in return? Only his dereliction.
The obscenity
Of his forgiveness.

THE UPPER ROOM

*from the tree-trunk sculpture of that name by Colin Wilbourn on
the riverbank below Durham Cathedral*

The river hauls itself round a slow
corner, a mud-coloured plate on which
reflections soften into laminar flow.
And that is time, gathering itself; time
gathers quite slowly towards Jerusalem.

Durham offers many parables – the fortress
Church, the dark recesses of God
into which dead saints are gathered.
And this household of shaved elms
by the river. The feast is quite simple –

here are the vessels we each are, part-
carved, sharing solidity with neighbours.
rivalry of height is mocked by his
sturdy sitting. On his left Judas –
no vessel, but a window – through him

every gale beyond Eden blows.
The world's weight gathers massive
upon a felled tree – time quickens
to a roar, drowning
strange words of blessing.

After towel and pitcher time will be flung
to a climax. This is the house of now,
ceasing to exist as the eleven leave,
the Master leading them,
and they sing their hearts away.

FOREIGN MISSION

In the years 1818 and 1819, about 5000 of the Cherokee Indians removed from their residence east of the Mississippi to a fine tract of country on the north bank of Arkansas River, between long 16 and 17 west. At their desire the American Board of Foreign Mission, have lately sent a mission family to teach them the arts of civilised life, and to instruct them in Christianity.

With what extraordinary civility the Cherokee, finding their previous residence rendered uncongenial by ethnic cleansing, deemed it convenient to settle on the north bank of the Arkansas – a sought-after plot, presently laid to forest, and not more than eight hundred miles from their home.

Their attitude, as recorded by the Commissioners, was in every way appropriate theologically as well as practically. They expressed a wish for a thing called civilisation, having previously had only settlement, agriculture and writing.

They asked for Christianity – difficult to grasp, this, but somehow they seemed to know that in the face of all the falsity of Federal words

they would need the story of a mocked god, a scourged silence before an unseeing Pilate.

The initial quotation is from Stephen H. Lang's *A Complete Historical and Geographical American Atlas, Being a Guide to the History of North and South America, and the West Indies* (Philadelphia: Carey and Lea, 1822)

MY SOUL LIKE A WEANED CHILD

The first verse is a quotation from Psalm 131.

I do not occupy myself with things
too great and marvellous for me.
But I have calmed and quieted my soul
like a weaned child with its mother;
my soul is like the weaned child that is with me.

My soul like a weaned child
sometimes held to me in such a bliss
of light on childish skin
as my soul takes her ease
at the edge of sleep
that on those days I have to watch only
in case some extravagant dream
float the infant so far
over cliffs of gold
that I cannot retrieve her from glory.

There are other days. They are characterised
by a racket of complaint –
if not actual food-flinging.

CAROLS AT THE MENTAL HOSPITAL

A band of imported choirboys
fill the unfamiliar, locked-all-year air
with carols. Once in royal..
The holly and .. the inevitable herald angels.

The singers tell the story that pure sound
can still transform musty space
into heaven. That there is still innocence
and possibility.

           Also that some souls
are born under fortunate stars,
sing in cathedrals,
and get saxophones for Christmas.

Others are consigned
to dingy air
to sweat out memories
of their last Nowell.

Masters of roll-ups.
           Abandoned of families.
Tellers of lifelines.
           Stumblers over life.

The angels are diplomats, then,
silent in waiting
when the hard question comes
as to why.

They dance a heralds' dance –
now on that treble's mop of curls,
now on the bankrupt farmer
in the front row,
now on the snooker-player next door,
icily picking off red and black,
red and black,
his named nurse watching.

What they herald is holly, dark and sharp;
blood dried black on a crowned head;
the sun obscured and the star stood still;
and royal-red memories woven without seam –

rolled up, flung down, turned.

RIDDLE

A man with iron-grey hair and glasses
Contemplates the cedar tree in the grounds.
He is a grizzly bear
He is a lover under the Cyprus moon
He passes his days at sketching and poetry.

A man with iron-grey hair and glasses
Paces up and down in a basement room
Talking to himself. In his right hand
A small grey object, tightly clutched.
He tells it a story, stops, tells it again.

I pass the two of them in the car-park.
The first man greets me warmly,
Presses my hand. The second
Does not seem to recognise me
Although we have met often.

I ask them both how things are..
'Grim', the first says. 'Miserable.'
The other (when pressed for an answer) 'Pretty grim.
They expect more and more from me,
Provide less and less.'

The two men talk once a week
At scheduled liaisons of ten resentful minutes.
The poet shouts, the other listens.
A sort of marriage exists between them.
Psychiatry is its name.

THE PATIENT IN THE CORNER

The river is slow, seems to drag
as though charged with an unbearable weight of silt.
His head, aimed at the floor, speaks
more than his dragged, silted words.
My talk is a cormorant's long dive after fish,
a wagtail's feathers flicking air.

Or – the river of him is in a cavern,
and I cannot see its surface,
or how attenuated light
glints on vortices of memory –
cicada-song, lime-blossom,
Pierrette in red. My talk is a gadfly buzzing.

His head aims at the floor,
he speaks
slow
reluctant
dragged-out
wisdom.

FUNERAL WIND

It was warm, for January, in a church
packed with overcoats paying their respects.
Dignitaries outdid themselves to search
for tributes – he had 'mastered many dialects
of learning', had 'taught the great', 'saw into the grain
of living', 'understood mystics', 'knew others' pain'.

He passed, in a plain box, out the South Door.
Children he'd loved had gathered there
awkwardly, as though still looking for more
of his smile. In the West Tower
bells hung silent. The wind, fierce from the north,
had no such scruple. It gave a cold greeting to death,

buffeting beaten trees in the churchyard,
the small party at the graveside. So hard
to concentrate on the last prayers – heart willing,
shoulders hunched at the cold. A killing
by cancer. A large spirit quenched. Tired earth
sheltered alone from an ill wind's mirth.

MISSION SANTA CLARA

At mass, on the thirteenth Sunday of ordinary time,
I find myself weeping for no reason I know.
I walk out into a strew of jacaranda flowers
like pale shreds of a purple cloak.

The garden is quietness, and placed light.
They lost eight from here, in El Salvador,
gunned down by Government order.

Ignatius in bronze reads his Exercises
to a fountain of struck rock, to oaks, catalpas,
olive trees from the days when this was Spain..

A chopper heads out for the coast.
Jacaranda leaves, delicate as a hawk's
flight-feathers, notice the breeze.

What does one remember
in the moment of martyrdom?
What place, what curve of love, what wave breaking?

What can I even begin to feel
protected by the Patriot Act
and the searching of my shoes at every airport?

The trees of the garden,
having taken breath, reply: wait –
wait till Ignatius turns the page.

IN MEMORIAM R.S.THOMAS

Your verse, a house of potent viruses –
Calvary, Kierkegaard, Prytherch –

Infected us, not with faith,
But with acceptance of a space of in-between,

A mountain-land where faith and doubt
Inhabit each other's shadow.

Your death leaves us still on the lower slopes,
Bereft of a good guide.

PATMOS

There is only ever our own fear, our own desire
warring in our heavens, wherever we
try to escape ourselves, wherever the fire
of sunrise meets us. Thus runs the theory.
So even John, on wind-weary Patmos,
caught in the cosmic symphony of his vision,
argued bitterly with his Ephesus
self, and fretted at his former friends' derision.

We may feel along the cavern floor for John's
finger-holds, or sing our praises on the beach,
or haunt some ouzo place, flaunting our tans.
It does not change the silver of which each
is made. But we can be woven by such a place,
or spun, or twisted, in this brief time of grace.

IONA

I come six hundred miles to be here –
exchange heather for heather, Dartmoor streams
for Sound of Mull. I come for sorting,
space, aloneness. I am content
when the mist falls
                    on Scotland to the east.

For centuries this place was used to bury kings.
Then it lay forgotten, island
among many of the Lords of Argyll.
The ferry now crosses, recrosses
as thousands come
                    to borrow misty peace.

How Columba would have wondered,
standing by his wattle cell, staring
into Scotland, the Christless hills.
This island of burial, memory, retreat
danced under his feet
                    like a springboard.

LINDISFARNE

I. How Aidan and his monks came to Lindisfarne

They saw the setting sun cast a gleam
Over low, sea-hugging cliffs of Farne.

They chose a windblown rock, mimicked
Blessed Iona. They built in oak.

They saw how play of sea-otters bettered
Joy. They bound to them the Trinity.

They chose simple ways, the Master's, fishing
For pagan souls. They spelled out Gospels.

They saw dark stones of their new shore baptized
By seeping tide, day on day, and still black.

They chose the gyring wind, harshness of Farne,
Joy. They bound to them the Trinity.

II. Coming to Lindisfarne

Early onto the windblown flats
to find the light
already gone from Farne
and on the holy island
church on church knocked down.
The wind whispers urgently
to the sand. The island
seems to shiver.
The sand whips in fast whispers
away across the beach
into the swallowing sea.

Cuthbert used to stand all night
waist-deep in water, praying.
I shall never know
that continuity of sea and flesh –
otters' acceptance,
gift of cormorant's fish;
but sense, from the wind on the stone,
how those early prayers hang stubborn
about the scattered Farne,
and bind unto myself, this day,
the threefold God of sea and sky.

IV LOOKING EAST AT SUNSET

CRICK, WATSON AND THE DOUBLE HELIX

A single insight made the Book of Life cohere,
Sent two men shouting into a Cambridge bar.
More slowly there steals upon us the power, the fear.

The X-ray from King's, and Chargaff's pairs,
Not one helix, but two, fugues on a common air;
A single insight made the Book of Life cohere.

An amazing future, suddenly laid bare –
New drugs, cheap insulin, strawberries all the year.
More slowly there steals upon us the power, the fear.

They were to find the grammar of genes trickier
Than expected, the syntax harder by far.
But a single insight had made the Book of Life cohere.

They could see the Nobel, and the patenting wars,
The complex hunger for profit, healing, honour.
More slowly there steals upon us the power, the fear.

It was all there, in the thin Cambridge beer,
The Text of Texts, laid ready for the sequencer,
A single insight made the Book of Life cohere.

Harder to take in the tears at the screening centre,
The many deaths of unborn others,
But slowly there steals upon us the power, the fear.

Now we face the uninsurable cancer,
Anticipate the repertoire of the baby-tweaker.
A single insight made the Book of Life cohere,
And slowly there steals upon us the power, the fear.

KNOWING

My first experiment on living tissue.
Pick a new leaf – copper beech –
chop into chloroform. Watch
as the hydrophobic pigments
leach to solvent.
A longer lesson is to follow those leaves
from bud-burst,
each morning after lovemaking,
savour their tints from pale strawberry
to old, tannic claret
and on into honey and on into rusted gold.

Dusk falls on the Sound of Sleat.
I feel, as much as see, the pulse
that is each new wave. Each is a pattern
duplicable in a ripple-tank.
Each is known, felt,
by the way it gathers out of Sleat
to beat on the Skye shore.
Gannets at their dusk feeding
stoop and plunge, piercing
the vibration as it runs for the rocks,
eloquent of time, eloquent of sadness.

Home. Above the beech-tree's blur
I trace star-shapes – swan,
dragon, chained maiden,
the same lion the Babylonians saw.
The stars are the frame, the ambit of our dreams
yet without Edwin Hubble's
patiently gathered spectra
we would not know their headlong retreat
from primordial densities
unpicturable

from our low-cubit vantage-point.
And humans have to be known
not only by our courteous kisses over wine,
the massive band-width of our communication
and the tuned nuances of the cat-walk,
but by the open hazard of the savannah –
eagles screaming overhead, baboons jeering,
the need for survival, the need for tribes,
ever the hankering
for Eden.

SANCTE ET SAPIENTER

*a poem in honour of the work of the Chapel at King's College, London,
for the Service of Thanksgiving for its Renewal, May 2 2001*

The task of this house is to be a lens
(In a place where light is categorised)
To gather up explorations
Bless them in humility.

In this same place, disciplined
X-ray looking into the Book of Life
First showed its code to be
A helical simplicity.

Such artistry.

            The Chapel's optical aids
Are wooden Job, and icons,
And a man-trap of beaten silver
Toothed with cruelty.

The gift of this house is to be a lens.
Its surfaces shine again today
As they did for Gilbert Scott
Bright-recollecting Italy.

And while he dreamed, vision
Gained its Theory of Everything –
Electromagnetism was etched
Into four lines of quiet clarity.

Such certainty.

            Twelve doctors monitor
Our focus here, familiar with pride,
And with the need for persistence
In prayer and polity.

The glory of this house is to be a lens,
Back-lit, accepting light
Into the desolate blue of the Lady
Into communion with agony.

Through a single piece of ancient glass
Falls the counter-image of wisdom
Spirit's other gift
The 'be-it-unto-me'.

*Note: This poem celebrates not only the X-ray crystallography of
Franklin, Wilkins and their colleagues at King's, the most influen-
tial experimental work in biology in the 20th Century (leading as
it did to the Watson-Crick structure for DNA), but also the
equations of James Clerk Maxwell, Professor of Natural Philosophy
at King's from 1860-65 and arguably the greatest theoretical
physicist of the 19th Century. Mary's robe in the central window
of the apse is made from the one piece of old English glass in the
new Chapel.*

REWEAVING THE RAINBOW

We have unwoven the glowing strands,
seen hope as multiple internal reflection,
measured indigo in Ångströms.

We know where to look for the Lord's sign –
always opposite the sun, at a certain angle,
the double bow above, and fainter,
(reversed, of course, since the light
as though losing its way on a roundabout
performs an extra pass of the rain's geometry.)

Knowing where to look

take a handful of soil from under a loved tree,
or dip your hands in a bowl of rosewater
tinctured with yew;

make the mark of the bow on a friend's hand.
Trace the seven colours of love there –
sense, fainter, what, between friends,
can never be spoken.
Feel the elements within you
stir towards the glow of freedom.

GETTING IT RIGHT

Standing in a waterfall's cave
and timing our first kiss
to meet the drops of spray placed by God
on your upturned lips.

*****

Emma Kirkby on the radio. *Kyrie.*
Glowing surge of liquid helium
over a vacuum rim
then filaments of thin air
given shape by risk,
eleison,
eleison.

*****

An old man, in a red sweater.
Carpark farewell statue to his daughter,
whose skirt swirls, who has dyed her hair
copper this time, who will glance back just briefly,
checking her blind-spot. He is the complete master
of their brief hug, of his timed wave
that just catches her glance,
of the shrug-free stumble
past the line of the shed, after which
he can safely howl.

TABOO

*Otto Hahn and Lise Meitner collaborated on the experiments that
led to the discovery of nuclear fission in 1938-9.*

It is in our bones, in the knitting of them,
In the assembly of our atoms
Into community. Taboo was there in Eden.
For one fruit glowed with forbiddenness;
On one tree, plain enough perhaps
To look at, which in spring had flowered
Like an outbreak of stars, or in blossoms
Fine as a flamingo's wing, but then
Was ordinary in leaf, half-hiding
The exquisite harvest – on that one tree
We may imagine concentrated all
The chantment of a world made by God –
All the left-over star-stuff of the cosmogoner.
So that to eat the faintly glowing fruit
Was to come a hair's breadth, a photon-burst too close
To the one who had formed all things. To be exposed
To a blast of possibility
Too vast to be contained within our frame.
Which we did, and have dealt since then –
Man to blamed woman, human to all
This glory-scattered planet – evil.

But what if the fruit
Revered, measured from an admiring distance,
Should then be found to fragment *of itself* –
To drip its star-stuff on the innocent?
It had been doing so for years, when Otto
Helped his Lise pack her bags for Sweden.

Even in the dull, static lab photo,
Two of them staring stiffly at the frame

From a suitable distance apart
You can see the respect, yes, but also
The intensity of their affection, Otto's
Sturdiness, Lise's passionate commitment –
Severe, brilliant, Jewish, banned.
He writes to her about her other luggage
And by the way that he – silly – cannot
Seem to separate product from carrier
In the tests on the slow-neutron block.
Poor man. He has put the answer into
The question, used a cider barrel to test
For apple-juice.
Lise, exiled from everything she knew,
Writes back – challenges, explains, confides
'A few private requests', especially
'My index card file'. She pushes him
To look clearly into the dark glass.
On an envelope he notes her suggestion
As to the energy release. That
Is the horror. And he cannot sleep,
And he cannot but – out here beyond
Eden, where there is no concealment –
Cannot but consider (knowing his species),
The taking of his own life.
For once we find the innermost kernel
Can be made to melt before our eyes
The world is filled with a deadly, tabooless searching,
Pressing life hard against the unmeltable sword.

Later, watching the neutrons do their work,
Brighter than the New Mexico sun, a man
Wrote that he had become death,
Quoting Krishna. We reinvoke our favourite
Myths to look for limits. The lovely world
Is full of dissipate enchantment
And of the toxins we have made of it –
To poison a lamb at two thousand miles,
To kill a river with a teaspoon's dose.

Bring on the myths, then, and let them play
In the violent sunsets of this man-fired world.
And let but one taboo remain –
Against the crushing of that respect
I see in Otto's photograph. The furled
Rose of love, unanatomised,
Allowed to be itself, the high meadow
Allowed its brief tossings of joy.
For thirty years they worked together,
Always staying late. When the chemistry went well
They would sing Brahms to each other.
And every night each
Walked back from the Institute alone.

Bring on the myths again, but let them never
Lose (worst mockery of all)
The sense of how love can suffer and forgive
And give its secrets up – from Stockholm
For a card file, from many Golgothas.
Releasing us – to play death with the whole
Soul-stuff of the world – or into peace,
The furrow worked as though a garden – the future
Hoped for, as though it might belong to God.

MEMORY

Surely, he said, you *must* remember
That first diazotisation,
The isolation of the fluoborate
And the trick we used to tritiate
To the requisite specific activity?

What I remember is that category
Of memory, which now is wrapped
Round you like a cocoon.
Every day you secrete a new thread
And reach out for the threads of others.

While we were still scientists together
I too carried around a chronology
Of life marked out in advances
Regular as poplar trees marching
Down a roadside in Northern France.

I find you used to write poetry
Gave up at sixteen, dissatisfied
At not immediately being Eliot.
I, always the slower one,
Gave up science at twenty-eight,

And turn out poems of memory;
My poplar trees are smeared out
Across a pointilliste field of light.
Categories, and the names of catalysts,
Fail me. I remember long talks

At evening, not quite drunk,
And concerts by the river, more than
The Triposes by which we earned them.
I remember what you said,
Having gone to King's and seen history –

'Francis Crick – the DNA man –
Was at the lecture – and spoke!!'
I remember the scent of my lab;
How yours was always cleaner,
Your cocoon of xeroxes more complete.

Our fields collide in our common concern
About God. I think perhaps you
Should have been the poet –
So elusive is your agnosticism.
I point you at documents.

Jesus was there – the Christ man –
And spoke.
You must remember.

WISDOM GATHERED AT HAWTHORNDEN CASTLE
IN HOLY WEEK

Stay away from balloons
When your pencil is sharpest.

Stay away from Monday, and strontium-90,
Stay away from beetles, gathering jewels in Eden.

There are always lovers too lovely to be loved;
There are always instants in the mist.

The alchemists all fade away;
This is already the curve to winter.

Lament all you like the diamond edge of time;
Spread your straw for the baby from eternity.

***

A stoker on the Berlin-Baghdad Railway,
A gypsy with a record for homicide,
A groupie in Prague
All join hands under the chill-filtered moon.

Weave their stories into a jackdaw's nest,
Smoke them out with *The Review of Books*,
Concede your wormholes to Aphrodite,
Save your tears for the Lamb, timelessly slain.

V ANOTHER CITY

Amsterdam

THE BEGUINEHOF

A cast of a woman praying. She was taught
by prayer. She was taught by Eckhart.
She was always an object of suspicion,
finding and giving refuge. Amsterdam
buys and sells, burns blithe around her.

The air of the courtyard
seems drawn into laminar flow, ordered
by the offices of prayer.
The quiet of it is the quiet under the canopy
of a deep forest in winter – the spirit of each Beguine

like a reaching tree,
sheltering.

Boston

THE BOY FROM ILLINOIS

He begins to write her a short love-letter
about how, coming up Beacon Hill
that morning, he saw the street glisten after rain
and shouted for joy

how later he saw her on a balcony
by Quincy Market, listening to jazz,
saw her lean back in her chair,
hands behind her head, watching him.

How he has always been a solitary tower
but that look made him feel
like a bridge, like water,
like silence

how he planned to take her through Harvard Yard,
home of many calculations –
amatory and quantum-mechanical,
and buy her the best pastrami sandwich in the world.

He writes of how he saw her turn
at the first pulse of a twelve-bar
saw her fingers beat on the wrist
of some man or other

and how he is the trembling air
through which vibrates the very gut of the blues
and he is the spent jet fuel
on the flight back to Peoria.

Chicago

LAST SNOW, OAK PARK

April 2003

It slips away out of a backyard
already planted up for sunflowers.

It huddles behind the newsstand
by the galvanised viaduct.

It is as black as it is white.

Banner headline: Baghdad Fallen.

Particulates from many engines
stud the last snow-piles,

stain, like blind-sight,
this bright imperial spring.

IN FRONT OF CHAGALL'S 'AMERICAS WINDOW'

Eyes rest, dissolve into a deep
Lucid blue, like a lead-lined
Mosaic of the sea at nightfall.

Eyes play on a primitive mouth
At a trumpet, a lifted gold megaphone
Out of a riot of blue.

A child of America stumbles at the tripwire.
For an instant the arc of her balance
Crosses Chagall's cascading light,

Points to the field-grey of the courtyard.
Leaded blue and luminous violet tumble together,
Buckle the upraised torch of liberty.

The child and the masterpiece are saved
By an arresting hand. The arc remains,
Printed on us as possibility.

Granada

LOS ARRAYANES, PALACE OF THE ALHAMBRA

The fish sleep. The pool is moonlight
on darkened glass. Lines of poetry
incised into mirrored walls.

Ambassadors to the Sultan
made to wait around the mirror pool
reported back to the world

that a prince at last had made stone
speak of tents, had slaked
his love for water and starlight.

Sunrise on marble, thin gold.
The breeze off the mountain ruffles
(only for a moment)

our upside-down image.
Pierced surfaces advance, recede,
declare themselves unreachable.

The breeze catches at the song
of lost odalisques, rivals beheaded.
The surface settles. The fish feed.

Madrid

Summer 2004

In Madrid my bags are X-rayed
continually. The mimosas are in flower;

short neat sub-machine-guns
cordon the public buildings.

A hundred days since the train bombs,
the twisted steel, the lachrymal air.

Picasso's 'Guernica'. A horseshoe roughly nailed
supports the neck of the trampled Christ.

Mounted police, batoned, cigarette-smoking,
stand guard over the Prado.

A woman falls, a woman flees.
The town was important, on the way to Bilbao.

A horseshoe is the shape of a Moorish arch;
a shape come round to itself.

Greek logic came back to Toledo
in translations from Baghdad

and someone somewhere is sifting plans,
patterning the logic of the next bombs.

A woman – Pia, Laila, Miriam –
keens to the sky

caught between some horned face
and some careful plan.

Mytilene

ON FINDING IT EASIER TO KISS SAPPHO THAN HELEN OF TROY

A shimmering tunic
fashioned out of filaments of gold.
A peasant skirt of pale green, matching her eyes.
Those eyes, brilliant, chatoyant,
a flame of sunrise flickering on ocean.

Helen's need was the desert blowing through the fields of the lost
as she reached for me with those long white arms
I cried out for her to stop
before I drowned in her.
What most men wouldn't give, she said,

and laughed, a sound full of lute-notes
and the casting of Astyanax from the walls.
In a swirl of purest grace
she strode to a waiting taxi, and was gone
into a land I dream of nightly.

In Sappho's arms, strong, a little bony,
I am anxious not to presume
but there passes between us
in the awkward electricity of our first touch
at least the recognition, shared,
that it is hard to make a line of poetry
sing
          that beyond the struggles and joys
of sex-lives – the green yearnings
fumbling, angular fulfilments –
is the common task of making the dance of words,
pleasing the same muse, ever-jealous Calliope.
Sappho's lips press mine, honey-rich,
salt as the breeze to Troy,
                         I drink deep
of ancient Mytilene, from which I know
that this mouth has loved many, and has loved only poetry,
and I pull reluctantly away.

Paris

A man in the best leather sandals
And a sensible scarf
Inches his way along the parapet
Of the Quai de Bourbon.

He turns at the first birch tree now
The breeze from the west
Is keener than it was.

The pile of unopened bills
On the Second Empire secretaire
Grows higher. His income is the interest
On moments:
              The day the sentries of the *Waffen-SS*
Left the Pont Louis-Philippe for ever;
The day Marie brought him cherry blossom;
Dinner when he talked with Sartre.

The year before he turned at the Pont Neuf
Last year at the second tree.
This year the first.
By these markers he sees time pass.

He turns, still talking with Sartre,
The waiter at the corner café makes him a small bow.
The woman who spoke to him
At the service for Marie, considers him,
And turns right with her terrier, across the bridge.
By these gifts, and the steep grey faces
Of the Hotel de Ville, by the remembered
Sheets of colour at the Sainte Chapelle,
Where he used to pray when no-one was praying,
And the expressionless river,
And a weekly phone call from his daughter at Yale
He receives his days.

76

Rhodes

HOUSES OF BREAD

A tiny red-tiled church.
Groins of veined stone hold an apse
which frames an altar. A candle
floating in a cup of water
flickers out its flame.

In Ottoman times this place
became the bakery for the Muslim poor.
Its chimney survives as a window.
The walls remember their service –
leaven and ash.

On the beach there is a bakery,
a kind of concrete shack
where a family turns out crusty
caraway-grained loaves, the locals'
daily sustenance.

The place sweats heat
catches the salt-spray
fuses it with woodsmoke, cinnamon,
patience, caraway,
ash and leaven.

ARTIST OF THE ISLAND SUN

The day is used up now, and the sun falls.
Its worshippers wriggle their bodies away, and the deck-chair man,
Who has seen everything, allows himself a moment
To consider the sea.

It develops a stripe of light, reddish, burnt gold,
Stretching from the west. As he thinks on this
The stripe draws in towards him,
Its colour deepens.

Where they suck back off the shingle
The waves clear a few feet of sand,
New-mint them in copper, more brilliant
Than a hero's shield-rim.

Now only twenty waves find the light,
Crinkle it, grow a film of running cream;
Now only ten – will the day be saved
For a mere ten slivers of white-edged fire?

The deck-chair man knows better.
He has foreseen it all – the last five waves
Surfaced with burning petrol, the shield-rim's
Glow extinguished.

The sun's final fall is a reactor in meltdown,
The Taj burning,
An ancient domed church
Turned to oil-lamp;

Lastly a circus tent that a slate-coloured cloud
Fails to hold, for all its ropes of crimson silk. The air smokes
With night's onset. The man rests, turning eastward;
Trade dictates he give birth again tomorrow.

Venice

AFTER CARNIVAL

Rooms I dreamed as high and light
are by great counter-weighted doors
stuck shut. Communiqués
of closedness shoved across floors
tell futile tales. Prayer thickens,
fear prevents. And candles gutter –
I know it by broken seeping shadow –
appeals, by post, to choose better.

There is a hopeless circling past
the shores of other palazzi. Grime
at water-level. Algal mud.
Beyond reach, grace in outline.
I float back towards your landing-stage,
low to the water, waiting out the gloom
for one laugh, one dayspring hint,
echoing a high, shadowed room,

waiting out the dark
to surprise a single smile
which might weave a curve
in sunlight, hint at an aisle
into an entrance-way into a loggia
giving onto a garden having a peach-tree
flowering in winter, before the flowers lift, drift, gust
down a fast-running channel to the sea.

HICKS'S STORY

Lord Marchmain in Brideshead Revisited, *revealing that his
Italian mistress is a British citizen, says: 'She is legally Mrs Hicks,
are you not, my dear? We know little of Hicks, but we shall be
grateful to him if it comes to war.'*

Her voice was deep, rich, laughing.
It said: if you are very sure
who you are
you can follow me into the rhythm
of the gondolier's oar
into infinite sunlight on skin.

He followed her through Carnival, through
his hoarded salary. It was worth it, every lira.
It was while watching her dry herself
after yet another bath in the big tub
she would fill with steam and oils, and once even
let him share, that he had his great insight.

(No need to explain that, later,
reporting to learned gatherings,
or how the idea had grown on him
in the craft markets, at Florian's,
and walking away an autumn
in search of Tintoretto.)

Then Cara told him, eyes down, taking small quick steps,
a crisp Alpine wind scouring the Piazzetta,
that there would be a child. Married him,
courtesy of the English Chaplain,
in a strange little wedding-cake of a chapel,
belonging to some grandee or other.

There was no identifying, later,
the moment of the deceit. No knowing if the child
had been a fiction. If even those first glances,
bent by light on water, had been strategy.
Venice, he read somewhere, had had nothing to sell
but herself, for two hundred years.

I met Hicks, finally, at the Royal Society.
A dinner for the fiftieth anniversary
of Hicks's Theorem. He was stiff with distinction,
until the wine told. 'I know little of Marchmain,'
he said, 'but I am glad he is dead,
and hope he suffered.'

VI THE STONE AND THE GARDEN

These poems were written in the sculptor Peter Randall-Page's workshop, and in the garden of Dartington Hall, while Peter worked on a new commission for the garden.

POET IN A SCULPTOR'S WORKSHOP

Words are held in their places
by hoists and cradles
by a sheer din
of sanding and shaving and polishing.

Perched on a waistcoat
of dust-saturated sheepskin
I start the task
of setting words free.

At once they cluster round marble
hang over blocks of oölitic limestone
seeking to be names
seeking to be catalogue.

I ease the gravity field further
and now words are dust
whipped out at an all-forgiving
stubbornly-flowering blackthorn.

At the edge of chaos, only the heaviest
words hold their ground – icosahedra,
archetypes, Plato. A ton of boulder
leans on a piece of two-by-four.

Words, at the limit, are a fine zest
in the unnameable universe
of stone becoming shape.
                    An hour of dreaming vanishes

into a faintly blurred sky.

TWO MAQUETTES

I am a rock, when work requires it.
Those expecting a hard surface
encounter one.

Anyone who probes at all further,
using a special drill
or a gentle question,

strikes different grain, broken, faulted,
strikes anxiety,
unprocessed pain.

Below that, sunlit, elusive memories
free-floating on a sea of grief.

****

I am a block of irregular marble
which a sculptor
touches with hands

more knowing than any lover's,
seeking to release
a perfect form. He calls it

'Human Being Fully Alive'.
Even experts dispute
the extent of his handiwork

in the unfinished study of me
presently on exhibit.

PULSE

He runs his hand down a hollow
between spirals, as though down the breastbone
of a lover. The stone surrenders
to the hand its secrets;
the sculptor has laid bare its trust.

He will strike statements out of granites
and sand them away. He will seduce
the grain of stone, insist on its complicity.

He'll align caressed facets of passive stone
with old axes of yew
across from a Monterey pine.
At the unveiling he'll deprecate tributes,
rest a champagne flute on the stone.

The garden will dapple the light
of a mid-life star
on a stone by a forgotten hand.

It will protect the stone with thistles,
with thorns, cacti, scorching sand,
from a sun that will grow and cool,
grow as it cools,
cause the oceans to boil.

At last the stone will slip back
into a fesic melt, into a nebula,
into a carbon-stained cometary snowball.

Across the slow pulse of the stone's thinking
cuts the sculptor's knowledge of this.

VII A SUITCASE OF LETTERS

A SUITCASE OF LETTERS

My mother, unsteady, pilots her limbs
Across her bedroom, drags something
Out of hiding, lifts it into my hands.

A suitcase, pre-war, straps of perished leather.
Scuffed, stained, surprisingly heavy.
Stamped with the initials of her long-dead father.

At her insistence I take the case away.
Her parents' letters – from 1913.
While they were engaged they wrote every day.

I open the case warily, as though
Starting to disarm a bomb. Expectation
Is its name. Held in limbo

For many years, my mother's hope
That I would one day write
Her mother's life. The scope

Of the commitment slows my hands
On the case, as one might touch
A new lover slowly, not knowing what bonds

Might be gathering, already, in desire,
Around held shoulders, wrists caressed
And the caressing fingers, as they steal fire.

'Beloved mine', a letter begins;
Beneath it ribboned piles of beloveds,
An intensity, across years, that spins

My mind beyond entanglement and fear –
This is a gift not just of connection

To where I came from: the young doctor
And his childhood friend, forming
A natural and appropriate social match –
Behind that a yearning

To be part of a new kind of reality –
The faded-ink beloveds
Seem like gift of opportunity –

Not binding me, but setting my own love free
To hope and reach for endurance
Beyond its stolen fire, its early sorcery.

I wonder now that my mother
Lifting more than she could lift
Could part so easily with such treasure.

LOVE LETTER FROM THE EXETER INSTITUTION

'Have you ever been here, beloved?
It is a musty mid-Victorian old place
Frequented by very old and dilapidated looking gentlemen.'
(An advanced young lady of 1913
She imagines hers to be the first love-letter
Ever written in the musty place.)

'This time yesterday' she writes
'You put me on the train
Back from Town. I loved your room
And wanted to touch all the books and chairs
So you could feel I had lived there
If only for an afternoon.

The beauty of wind and sun and rain
Have never failed me yet, and I hoped
As I walked at Duryard
Where we became what we are
That the comfort of these things
Passed through my spirit into yours.'

She blushes as she writes,
And refuses a suggestion of her mother's
That *she* finish the letter off.
A fresh cream envelope.
She seals her love away
Forever from the musty air.

THE LETTERS

read on retreat at Hawthornden Castle

I immerse myself in their world –
The letters are my music in an isolated time.
They wait for me
On the hall-tables of my days
And through them I track the cadences
Of a long friendship.

How slow they were to give their feelings names.
In her journal, at eighteen, she writes that they 'fell behind'
While out riding – deep in an argument –

And rode six miles alone together, which some
Might consider shocking – but those people would be wrong;
Men and women should be able to be friends.

She writes that there is a new quality to her life.

Five years later they are still arguing, by letter,
Now about a 'Kathleen' who he made everyone feel
(she says) was the only woman in the room to him.

The fate of their dance – and of my genes –
Rests in the balance.

In retrospect she can write: 'I loved you then
And was proud and glad of it', but months pass
Before 'you told me that I mattered to you'.

The letters are ninety years old. All the people
Mentioned have died, bar one small baby
'astoundingly plump and healthy'.

They are my music here – an Edwardian
Improvisation on a well-worn theme –
Fresh, fragile, exploratory:

Being laid down in my memory like tree-rings.

INSULIN

The bite of surgical spirit, across the scent
Of drawing-room lilies. The clink of a glass
Hypodermic. A metal bowl among
The silver trays for visiting cards
And tea ceremonies. Terse, edgy tones
From the grown-ups. The over-careful
Pronunciation of a word, 'in-sul-in'.

Later I reran, at the expense of a wrung
Chicken's neck, the experiment that shows
Reversal of the effect of glucagon
In the liver. Safe stuff, in the chicken.
Making me feel I knew something,
Understood the family plague. My callow
Comment: 'a good biochemical disease'.

A good biochemical distance
From heartbreak. Lilian's brother at eleven,
Her father at forty-one. A son of ten
Starved in a London hospital, while more and more
Units of the strange new drug were tried.
Hubert, though a doctor himself, near to giving up
On the anguish, very near to saying

Let him eat what he likes.
But pulls back. *We know what would happen
Then. Whereas we don't yet know
What insulin will do.* The boy lives,
Is about to go out on a Cornish beach –
Bucket and spade, sisters, spaniel,
When the wire comes. Hubert, at forty.

His death certificate in my hand.
Did he know, before the collapse,
The coma, what was coming?
To increase, fractionally, our knowing,
I sit in labs to have my genes mapped,
Listen to the kick of this family's blood
Through the artery at my elbow.

My parents inject from disposables.
They stare at digital read-outs
From pin-pricks. Their insulin,
Genetically engineered now,
Remains mysterious, unpredictable friend,
Constant companion in cool-boxes,
Ally and spectre and memory.

FORMS

In this space
        on the baptismal certificate of 1889
State the quality, trade or profession
Of the child's father.

(Victorian quality assurance.)

In these spaces
        on the marriage licence of 1913
State the rank or profession
Of the fathers of groom and bride.

(Those fathers again.)

'Gentleman' and
'Gas engineer deceased.'
(More money, though, in the gas.)

In this space
        on the death certificate of 1926
State the causes of death in order of importance.

Diabetes Mellitus, the family plague
Undiagnosed in advance of
Coma – sudden, leaving so much unsaid.

Identify the informant.
Lilian, *'present at the death'.*

Do not state the numbness of it
Or the plans overturned.
Do not characterise the blur of feeling
From emptiness to guilt.

Say rather that the great adventure
Was remade, in another place,
With ponies and goats and bee-keeping,

And that she kept, quite incorrectly,
For forty-six more years,
Her dead husband's initials.

THE NEW START

She chooses a house that looks out to the hills,
that flings its windows wide and streams out
into summer meadows, furls itself close,
ancient, against the rains of winter.

On a certain autumn morning she rises early,
slides back the bolt, hearing the leaded lights
jump in their frames. She walks in easy shoes
down the gravel path, past the sundial.

This winter she will plant oaks in Front Meadow
which I shall know as the spreading trees of my
old age. But I am not in mind. She thinks
no dynastic thoughts, this filmy Devon dawn.

She bought the house for the bridge over the stream –
for its stone balls, reminder of Clare,
her husband's college. This is the past
receiving its due loyalty.

She watches a fox, pale as the morning,
cross the meadow. The sheen of his tail
caresses the air.
He is the alert present.

At the bridge she turns,
her eyes drawn from the line of the lily-pond
to whitewashed cob walls, thatch
sheltering under the sheltering hill,

then sees her daughter, who is ten, steal
from her window, walk in her own thoughts
down towards the river. This is the future;
Lilian savours it, against her loneliness.

The young girl, my mother, is past eighty now.
I stare out at the same meadow.
This assembling of hints and memories
comes to be a vital part of the peace-talks

between my own past and future.

FIAMMETTA IN HER TOWER

Seventy. For her birthday
her daughter sends her a love-story
about an Italian princess.
Lilian copies out a passage,
Fiammetta yearning to find
'in the familiar room
so long endeared by peaceful use
an enclosure against the unending solitude
by which she felt herself surrounded.'

She created, all her life,
by peaceful use, spaces clear and light,
simply adorned, full of flowers,
and filled her house for thirty years
with those needing refuge –
single mothers, brattish teenagers,
the difficult old.
                    An unending trail, travail,
scattering the space with rose-petals
torn and crushed.

I read now the messages
hidden in the chess-pieces of decorated bone,
the scrupulously-concealed cost
of holding the space, when no-one could any longer see
the young visionary, firebrand, lover
within the gracious lady.

I see her flow out onto her balcony
to stare into the rain-soaked hills.
She is again twenty, and loves by the filmy light
of the Cote d'Azur. She is Fiammetta in her tower.
She finds no space is proof
against the loneliness
of not being recognised as herself.

HER ANNIVERSARY BOOK

A life lived across two world wars:

John 'drowned in Egypt on active service';
Teddy 'dead in his submarine,
on his twentieth birthday';

lived too through an era
precarious for infants –
'she survived ten hours', he 'three days'.

But it is the book's last entry that holds me –
that on a certain day in October,
two years before she died,

Lilian went up onto the moor
with her dead daughter's friend, to scatter her ashes
in a place the two had loved.

A woman of eighty-two,
on the arm of one of forty,
in ritual action, across decades and outlooks –

appropriate action (like the patiently-noted, appropriate presents
                                                 to godchildren)
with a void behind it
of crushed hope and unexpressed farewell.

She notes without comment
that it was 'the day Nutmeg went' –
the daughter's much-loved grey.

How matter-of-factly
a long life fills up with loss.

EARLY JOURNAL AND LAST LETTERS

I. *Penseroso*

1906.
I have often thought how much I should like to read
all about my doings and feelings as a school-girl
when I am quite an old woman.
Then it will be for me to read over these pages, now so white and clear..
I have left my time-table in..
I think it will amuse me,
to see how my life was divided up into half-hours.

1973.
The old Bishop of Marlborough
prepared me for confirmation,
almost seventy years ago now.
What if, I asked him, what if religion
Seemed suddenly unreal and useless?
Go on saying your prayers, he said,
And in time life will come back to them.

II. *Cantabile*

(sixteen)
Fanny has got so grown-up and proper.
I wonder if I shall
when I put my hair up –
somehow I don't think so.

(seventeen):
what I feel for H I do not know,
but I am certain it is not love – I feel exactly like a real friend.

(eighteen):
once more happiness is the burden of my song.
I have given H permission
to use my Christian name.

(engaged to be married)
Beloved, sometimes I play little lonely notes
on the piano, just to remind myself
of the sounds, and then I want
very much that you should be there playing
and I should be watching your
quick fingers
and listening.

(widowed forty-six years)
Music endures – the Preludes and Fugues,
the St.John Passion. How my husband
would have loved to have heard
the recording quality of the 1970s.
It was so relatively poor in his time.

III. *In the curious intimacy of reportage*

1913.
Everyone is most amused at the idea
of Lilian being engaged. They ask her
if she has given up being a suffragette
and doing good works...

1972.
The last four weeks have exhausted her.
She feels the virtue has gone out of her
and she has little left to give.

Sunday morning.
Took dogs up on the Gorge
and cooked a chicken for luncheon.
Just remembered Christopher's birthday
in time
and sent him some gloves.

CODA

I close the suitcase – it and the letters
are attic-bound. They leave their myths
behind, their tenderness –
The delight of those days and nights
at Crackington Haven, and now the clothes
of our baby-child, lying in their basket,
waiting to be worn.
Their harshness, and penitence:
I deserved the bitter letter
and will try, if you will help me,
to make things less hopeless
in the future.
They say long friendship can be consummated
in passionate, unregretting belief.
And that years can lose patience
with what was once longed for.

He died suddenly, at forty.
She made a new life for herself.

Pasteboard announcements of marriages and deaths
crumble at the edges, blacken,
give off a fine dust when touched.
The myths fuse with my own –
antimony with tungsten,
silver with mercury.
An edge now to my tenderness,
a richness to my sternness,
a reach to penitence – that, and hope, persist.

FLOWERS

'I do not think I have ever seen anything so lovely as this bluebell.
I know the beauty of our Lord by it.' (Gerard Manley Hopkins)

'You will always burn flowers, won't you? I would hate to be left
to wilt and wither, and then be thrown on some heap or other.'
(Lilian Willey to Hubert Depree, 1913)

Flowers press on me from every side.
From old photographs they stare out
A passionate vision of a changed world.
They grin at their lover
Struggling with an early camera.
They gaze thoughtfully from a high place,
Past conquered summits, down to an Alpine valley.

They bloom with such energy, such flourish.
Before their fragrance my heart fails.
By them I know the creator's genius
And his irony.

This winter I hear the stories of flowers
At a stream of funerals, seeming incessant.
They had such hopes. He rose rapidly...
They opened their house to the arts...
She fashioned space, and atmosphere...
They never really recovered from...
The withering process that is life.

Another bloom of pre-war tennis-parties
Is honoured in chill air
By a huddle of overcoats.
Above the grave a stubborn magnolia buds.

MY MOTHER'S PLATO

My mother's Plato
expectant on my desk.
Page on page of Greek characters
like flocks of birds
flowing and turning across a big sky.
Footnotes in Latin.

I open the codebook hopefully,
run my fingers over texts.
They are a kind of Braille for excellence,
cipher for a shy intimacy
to which the key
is lost for ever.

In our fifty years I never got beyond
the opening call-signs, first few
guesses at positions
on the beautiful and the good.
Hers was a difficult music
often misconstrued.

I pick out words
in her lexicon,
miss – long for –
their articulation,
their taking flight.

A MONTH AFTER HER DEATH

We are all experts on our memories.
I elide the blood-apricot moon of my mother's dying
with last night's yellow, jazz moon,
reorganise them like a chess defence,
a Grünfeld against grieving.
On every board but one
it works
          for I have made it hard
to spot the opening. A shy boy sees it,
remembers journeys,
                    notices a Japanese magnolia
come into flower, hears the cadence
of being taught its Latin name.
I offer him my resignation, move from board to board,
flick clock after clock. The boy is too stubborn
to accept. He sets my defences upright,
destroys them again and again.

TULIP TREE AT GLENDURGAN, AUTUMN

for my mother

You set yourself, beyond the last
of your strength, to walk
the whole length of the ravine,
past the tulip tree, across the maze,
down to the distant sea.
You walk in the persistence
that is your creed, lean heavily
on my arm.

Tulip leaves, prayers escaping their bindings,
fall carefree yellow,
lie thick, stained gold.
I could never tell what you were thinking,
which leaf of your mind shone
with the placed sunlight of your thought;
that day perhaps it was Xenophon
or the *liliodendra* we saw in Savannah.

In my memory I am talking
to keep my spirits up. You are doing
what you set yourself to do.
What you taught me
was always to look beyond the maze,
thalassawards,
always to take a chance
on the music of the distant sea.